Fats

by Rhoda Nottridge

Carolrhoda Books, Inc./Minneapolis

All words that appear in **bold** are explained in the glossary on page 30.

Photographs courtesy of: Bryan and Cherry Alexander, p. 15; Bruce Coleman, pp. 4, 11, 23; Eye Ubiquitous, pp. 10, 13, 29; Science Photo Library, p. 16; Wayland Picture Library, pp. 8, 21; Zefa, pp. 5, 6, 25, 26.

This book is available in two editions.
Library binding by Carolrhoda Books, Inc.
Soft cover by First Avenue Editions
241 First Avenue North
Minneapolis, Minnesota 55401

First published in the U.S. in 1993 by Carolrhoda Books, Inc.

Library of Congress Cataloging-in-Publication Data

Nottridge, Rhoda
  Fats / by Rhoda Nottridge
    p.   cm.
  Originally published: Wayland Publishers : Hove, East Sussex, 1992. Includes biographical references and index.
  Summary: Introduces different types of fats, explains why they are both useful and harmful to the body, and discusses ways to cut down on unhealthy amounts of fat by eating correctly and exercising. Includes recipes and activities.
  ISBN 0-87614-779-1 (lib. bdg.)
  ISBN 0-87614-606-X (pbk.)
  1. Lipids in human nutrition—Juvenile literature.
[1. Fat.] I. Title.
QP751.N68   1993
613.2'8—dc20   92-26758
                                                    CIP
                                                     AC

Printed in Belgium by Casterman S.A.
Bound in the United States of America

1 2 3 4 5 6 98 97 96 95 94 93

Contents

What Is Fat?

We all need lots of **energy**, especially when we are growing. Fats, which are in many foods, can give us up to twice as much energy as other kinds of foods. Fats give us the energy we need to stay alive.

Our bodies store fat under the skin. This body fat keeps

BELOW *We need some fat in our diets to give us energy. Fats inside our body help us stay warm.*

us warm. Body fat around our eyeballs and other body parts cushions them so they are less likely to be damaged.

Fats we eat also give us **vitamins** A, D, E, and K, and some important **minerals**. We

need these to keep us healthy.

Fats add flavor and texture to food, making things more tempting to eat. A meal that contains fats also helps you to feel full longer, because fat stays in your stomach for quite a long time.

There are solid fats, such as butter, and liquid fats, such as cooking oils. We can see fats called visible fats in some food. In bacon, the fat is the white part between the strips of red meat. On fried foods, you can see the grease because it makes the food shiny.

In some foods, such as milk, it is not so easy to spot fat. The hidden fats are called invisible fats. Quite a lot of the food you eat contains fats that are invisible. Many of your favorite foods, such as chocolate candy, nuts, ice cream, cookies, salad dressings, and other **processed** foods, all contain hidden fats.

ABOVE
French fries contain at least 5 percent fat. You can see it shining on the fries.

Nearly all liquid fats are kinds of vegetable oil. These oils come from the seeds of some plants. Solid fats, such as butter, are made from dairy products or from the meat of animals.

BELOW *Ice cream contains invisible fats.*

Science Corner

You cannot always tell if a food contains fat simply by looking at it.
Here is an experiment to help you find invisible fat in foods.

You will need:
2 pieces of paper towel
1 slice of tomato
1 piece of cheese

1. Lay out two pieces of paper towel or parchment.
2. Gently rub a piece of cheese against one piece of paper.
3. Now gently rub a slice of tomato against the other piece of paper.
4. Remove the slices of cheese and tomato. Leave the papers to dry.
5. When the papers are dry, there will be a grease stain where the
   cheese was rubbed and no grease stain where the tomato was rubbed.
   This shows that cheese is a fatty food and that tomatoes do not
   contain fat. You can try this experiment with any food to see if
   it has invisible fats.

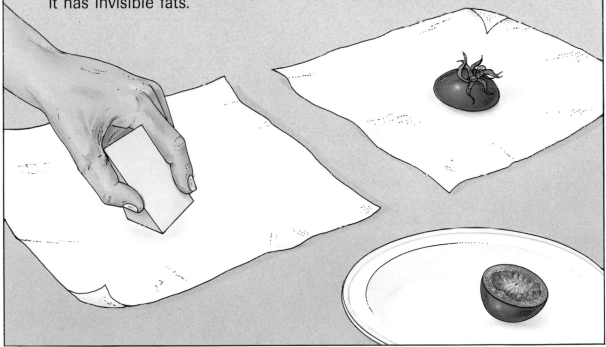

Fat Facts

We have learned to sort fats by how they look—solid or liquid, visible or invisible. But there is also a way to sort fats by the way they are put together and the way our bodies use them. If you want to look after your health, you need to know about these differences among fats.

The diagram on page 9 shows how to sort fats and oils into two main groups. These groups are called **saturated** and **unsaturated** fats and oils.

BELOW *Vegetable oils, animal fats, dairy products, fruits, and nuts all contain different kinds of fats.*

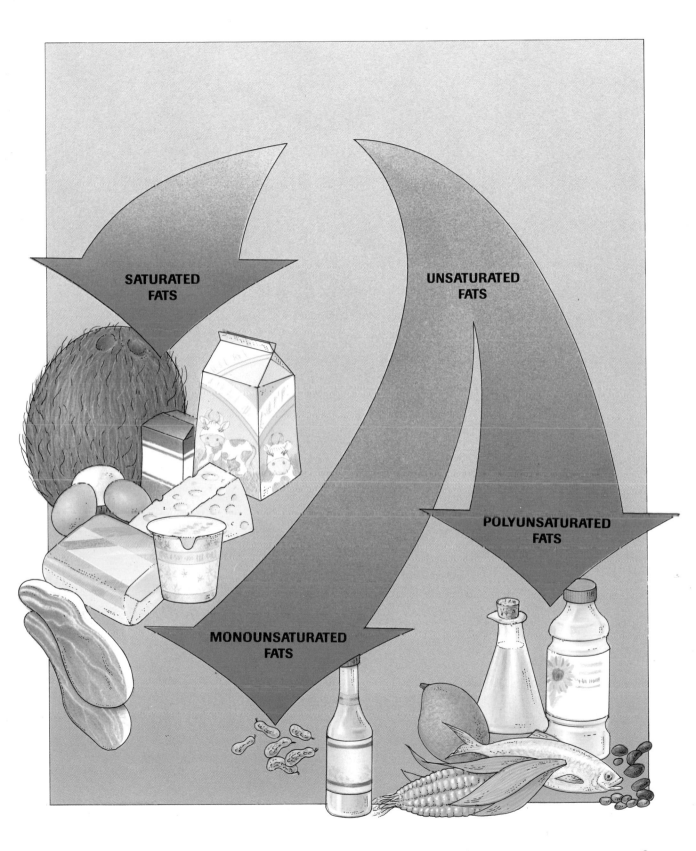

SATURATED FATS

UNSATURATED FATS

POLYUNSATURATED FATS

MONOUNSATURATED FATS

to be high in saturated fats. Too much saturated fat in your **diet** can be bad for your health.

Unsaturated fats can be divided up further into **poly-unsaturated** and **mono-unsaturated** fats. These fats usually come from parts of plants, such as their seeds, fruit, or vegetables. Only a dozen or so types of plants are commonly used to make vegetable oils. These include sunflowers, soybeans, grapes, and olives.

Most fats and oils contain both saturated and unsaturated fats. But most fats contain more of one type than the other.

Most of the foods that contain a lot of saturated fats come from animals. These fats include milk and milk products, eggs, and the fats that can be seen in meat. Saturated fat is often used in processed foods, such as cakes and cookies, because it does not spoil as quickly as unsaturated fats. Coconut oil and palm oil also happen

ABOVE *Olive oil is high in monounsaturated fat. Olive oil is made by pressing the fruit of the olive tree to squeeze out the oil.*

How can we tell which type of fat we are eating? We can make a good guess simply by looking at how hard, soft, or liquid a fat or oil is. At room temperature, corn oil is a liquid. It is high in polyunsaturates. This means it contains much more unsaturated than saturated fat. At room temperature, beef fat is hard. It is also a highly saturated fat. The harder a fat, the more

BELOW *Oil from sunflower seeds is high in poly-unsaturated fat.*

likely it is to be high in saturated fats. The softer a fat is, the more likely it is to be unsaturated.

Of course, there are some exceptions to this rule. Some fats are processed at food factories, so that what you buy as a hard fat may once have been a liquid fat. The best way to know what you are eating is to read the label, where all the ingredients are listed.

Science Corner
Quick Bean Bonanza: A polyunsaturated salad
This tasty salad uses polyunsaturated oil.

You will need:
1 15-ounce can of
    kidney beans
½ green pepper
1 apple
2 stalks of celery

For the salad dressing:
2 teaspoons sunflower oil
1 teaspoon lemon juice
½ teaspoon mustard
pinch of black
    pepper

First prepare the salad dressing:
1. Put the oil, lemon juice, mustard, and pepper into a clean screw-top jar.
2. Make sure the lid is screwed on securely, then shake the mixture until the oil and lemon are mixed together.

For the salad:
1. Drain and rinse the kidney beans and put them in a large bowl.
2. Carefully wash the celery, apple, and green pepper. Cut the celery into thin slices. Cut the core out of the apple and the seeds and stem out of the pepper. Chop the rest of the apple and green pepper into small pieces.
3. Mix them all together in a bowl with the salad dressing.
4. Eat and enjoy!

Make sure there is an adult nearby when you are cooking.

The Heart of the Matter

The heart is actually just a muscle the size of a fist. It works day and night to pump blood around to every part of the body. Blood travels to and from the heart through a network of tubes, called **veins** and **arteries**.

Our blood carries oxygen from our lungs to all parts of the body. It also collects **carbon dioxide**, which the body makes, our blood brings it back to the lungs for us to breathe out. Our blood needs fats in it to help it flow to all these places in the body.

There are different types of fat in our blood. One of the important types is called **cholesterol**. Our bodies need cholesterol. We can get it from eating saturated fats, or our bodies can make it for us. Our liver makes cholesterol and other important chemicals for us.

LEFT *Jogging speeds up your heartbeat. This exercises your heart to make it stronger. It also causes blood to be pumped through your arteries faster. This reduces the chance of fats sticking to the artery walls.*

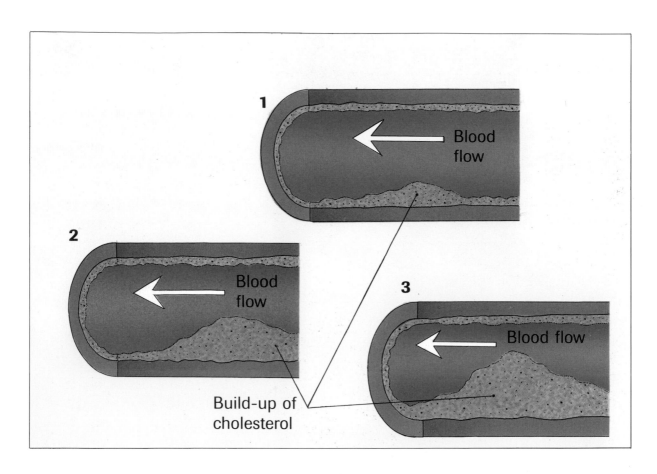

1

Blood flow

2

Blood flow

3

Blood flow

Build-up of cholesterol

If your body has too much cholesterol in the blood, your body will normally get rid of the extra fat as waste. Some people's bodies are not able to do this. The amount of cholesterol in their blood stays high.

If you have too much fat in your blood, the fat starts to stick to the inside of your arteries. This narrows the tubes that carry blood around your body.

If the tubes leading to the heart narrow too much, the heart does not get enough blood—or oxygen. This can cause a **heart attack**.

Heart attacks can also be caused when an artery is blocked by a **blood clot**. Sticky blood containing too much fat can cause a clot to build up in a tube.

You can have your blood tested to see how much cholesterol it contains. If people have a lot of fat in their blood, they need to cut down on the amount of fat they eat.

They also need to make sure that the fats they do eat are high in polyunsaturates rather than high in saturates. This is because the fats that are the most likely to stick to arteries come from saturated fats.

To keep our hearts healthy, we all need to change to eating more polyunsaturated fats instead of saturated fats. The Inuit people of Greenland and the fishing people of Japan are less likely to have heart problems than people in the United States or Europe. This is because of the foods they eat. Although they eat a lot of fat, most of it comes from fish, which is high in polyunsaturates. And people who use a lot of olive oil in cooking are also less likely to have heart disease. Olive oil is a monounsaturated fat.

People in the United States and Europe eat too much of all kinds of fat. Nearly half of the energy we get from food comes from fat. That means we eat over 3 ounces of fat each day. The amount of fat we eat should be only one third of our diet, or around 2.5 ounces a day.

Other parts of the way you live also affect how likely you are to have heart problems later in life. For example, jogging regularly and never smoking will keep your heart healthier. When you exercise, your blood is pumped quickly through your arteries. Sticky fats have less

BELOW *The Inuit people of Greenland eat a lot of Arctic Char, a type of fish that is high in polyunsaturated fat.*

ABOVE *All of these foods contain fats. We should only eat about 2½ ounces of fat each day.*

chance to stick to the sides of the tubes.

Exercise also makes all your muscles strong and healthy, including your heart. Good exercises for your heart include jogging or running, skipping, bicycling, swimming, cross country skiing, and badminton.

Jog for joy!

Jogging means running at a slow, comfortable pace, breathing regularly. Try to jog on soft ground, such as grass, rather than on a hard surface, such as concrete. Make sure you wear running or exercise shoes that cushion your feet.

Every time you go jogging, you need to do some warm-up exercises first. Bend and stretch every part of your body in turn, as if you were stretching during a yawn.

Have a healthy heart!

Here's a program to slowly increase how long you can exercise without getting out of breath and feeling tired. Each week, do the amount of exercise suggested three times that week. By the time you get to the sixth week, you will be able to jog for 20 minutes. If you feel any pain or discomfort during jogging, stop immediately and talk to your coach or physical education teacher about it.

	walk briskly	jog	walk briskly
WEEK ONE	10 min.	2 min.	10 min.
WEEK TWO	4 min.	3 min.	3 min.
WEEK THREE	7 min.	6 min.	7 min.
WEEK FOUR	4 min.	12 min.	4 min.
WEEK FIVE	1 min.	18 min.	1 min.

Quiz

Do you eat too much fat?
Read the questions and write down the number of points you score for each question on a piece of paper.

points

1. *What type of milk do you drink?*

whole milk	3
low-fat (2 percent) milk	②
low-fat (1 percent) milk	1
skim milk	0

2. *How often do you eat fried foods, such as french fries, fajitas, fried chicken, or egg rolls?*

every day	3
once or twice a week	2
less than once a week	①
hardly ever or never	0

3. *How often do you eat chocolate, cake, or cookies?*

every day	3
once or twice a week	2
less than once a week	①
hardly ever or never	0

4. *How often do you eat cheese?*

every day	3
once or twice a week	②
less than once a week	1
hardly ever or never	0

5. *How much fat, such as butter or margarine, do you spread on bread, toast, or rolls?*

a thick layer	3
a medium amount	2
a thin scrape	1
none at all	0

6. *How often do you eat foods like potato chips, cheese puffs, or nuts?*

every day	3
once or twice a week	2
less than once a week	1
hardly ever or never	0

7. *How often do you eat sausages, hamburgers, or other kinds of pork or beef?*

every day	3
once or twice a week	2
less than once a week	1
hardly ever or never	0

Now add up your score.

If you scored 14 or more, you are probably eating too many fatty foods. Try to cut down on fried foods and fatty snacks. Instead, eat more fresh fruit and vegetables, and make sure you get plenty of exercise.
If you scored between 7 and 13, you eat a reasonable amount of fatty foods, but be sure you're aware which foods are less fatty.
If you scored 7 or below, well done! You have a diet that is low in fat. As long as the food you eat is varied, you should be feeling fit and healthy.

Choosing Fats

Too much meat?
You can control how much fat you eat by choosing your diet carefully. Meats such as liver, salami, bacon, and ground meats like hamburger tend to be very fatty. White meats, such as chicken and turkey, are less fatty. Some people cut out all meat from their diets.

BELOW White meats such as chicken have less fat in them than red meats and most processed meats.

Choosing cheeses
Cheeses are often high in fat. The best way to cut down on this kind of fat is to eat a different kind of cheese. Cheddar and blue cheese are high in fat, Brie and Edam contain less, and cottage cheese is a very low-fat cheese.

Is butter better?
It takes the cream from more than 5 quarts of milk to make .5 pound of butter. Cream is very high in fat, and therefore so is butter. Butter contains vitamins A and D, and salt is often added to it. People have made and eaten butter for centuries.

Margarine and spreads
Margarine is made from either a mixture of animal and vegetable oils or just from vegetable oils. Most margarines contain the same amount of fat as butter. Margarines made with sunflower or soybean oil are better for your health because they are high in polyunsaturates.

particularly important for the healthy growth of teeth and bones.

You can choose how much fat is in the milk you buy. The different types of milk are called whole milk, low-fat milk, and skim or nonfat milk. Whole milk has had nothing added to it and nothing taken away. It is about 3.5 percent fat, the same amount of fat as when it left the cow. It is good for young children, although it is too rich for small babies.

Low-fat milk has much less fat because most of the cream has been removed. The label tells how much fat is left, 2 percent, 1 percent, or less.

To be called margarine, a product has to be almost all fat. There are now many spreads that are much lower in fat. Some contain as little as 20 percent fat. These are useful for spreading, but can't be used in cooking.

Which milk?
Milk is an excellent drink that contains **proteins**, vitamins, and minerals. One of the minerals it contains is calcium. Calcium is

ABOVE *It takes the cream from this much whole milk to make a piece of butter this size!*

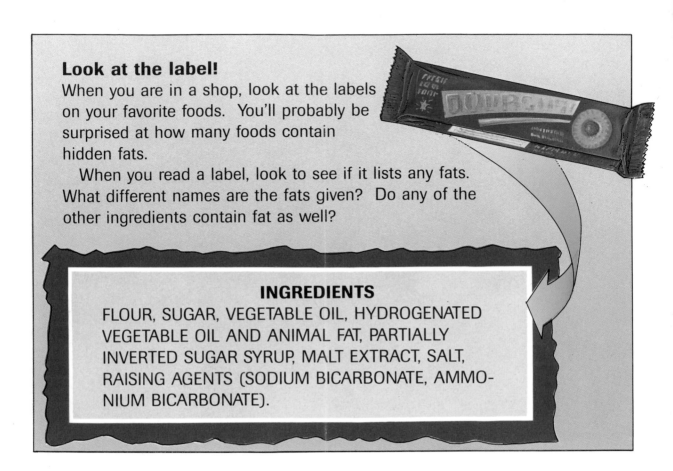

Look at the label!

When you are in a shop, look at the labels on your favorite foods. You'll probably be surprised at how many foods contain hidden fats.

When you read a label, look to see if it lists any fats. What different names are the fats given? Do any of the other ingredients contain fat as well?

INGREDIENTS

FLOUR, SUGAR, VEGETABLE OIL, HYDROGENATED VEGETABLE OIL AND ANIMAL FAT, PARTIALLY INVERTED SUGAR SYRUP, MALT EXTRACT, SALT, RAISING AGENTS (SODIUM BICARBONATE, AMMONIUM BICARBONATE).

Many of the vitamins were removed with the cream, but they have been added again. Low-fat milk is not suitable for young children, but it is a healthy choice for the rest of the family.

Skim milk has almost all of the fat removed. Less than .5 percent of the milk is fat. It is not rich enough for children under five. The label tells which vitamins have been added back to make up for the ones that were taken out with the fat.

OPPOSITE
Milk straight from the cow is full of calcium and vitamins. It also contains a lot of fat.

Science Corner

Strawberry Shake

Drinks can be just as good when they're made with low-fat milk. Try this recipe for a less fatty milkshake.

You will need:
1 cup chilled low-fat milk
1 8-ounce carton of low-fat strawberry yogurt
a few fresh strawberries if available

1. Pour the yogurt into a bowl and add the milk.
2. Use a whisk or fork to mix the two together.
3. Pour into a glass and decorate with a strawberry.
4. Serve immediately.

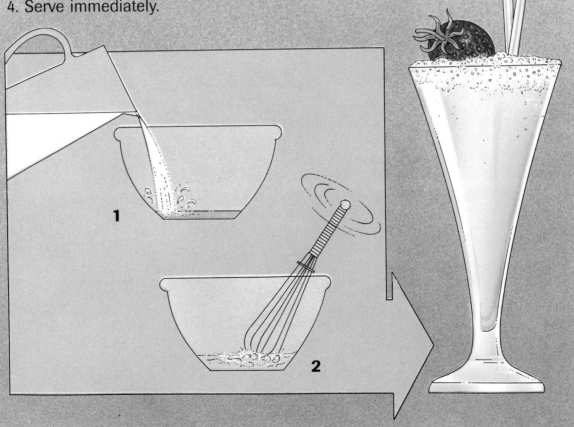

Too Fat, Too Thin?

ABOVE *Fresh fruits and vegetables have a lot of vitamins, minerals, and other good things in them.*

Young people need to get plenty of energy from their food. Adding inches to your height means building new bones and muscles, and that takes extra food energy.

We all need to eat a mixture of foods. If you eat only a few kinds of foods, you may not get all of the vitamins, minerals, or other things you need to stay healthy. You should eat plenty of fresh fruit, vegetables, and cereals, and not too much sugar or fatty foods.

When people are overweight, their hearts must work harder, which is not healthy. Unhealthy eating habits, lack of exercise, or other factors may cause a person to be overweight.

One way for overweight people to thin down is to slowly start exercising. They may also need to change their eating habits. Too

ABOVE *Some people can't see themselves the way they really are.*

OPPOSITE *Regular exercise will help you to keep your body trim and healthy.*

much sugar and too many fatty foods may cause a person to gain weight.

Quick "crash" diets can harm your health. People who lose weight on quick diets usually gain it right back as soon as they stop dieting.

Before someone tries to lose weight, he or she should talk to a doctor or a health teacher to find out the best way to do it.

Many people worry that they don't look right. You may think you are too tall or too short, too thin or too fat. As you grow, your body changes shape. Some people put on weight and then slim down as they grow taller.

It is important not to be too worried about your weight. Some people think they are too fat when they are not, and may try to stop themselves from eating. They even starve themselves and can become seriously ill.

Other people may eat far too much whenever they are unhappy, thinking it will cheer them up. They often feel bad about this and may even make themselves throw up the food.

These eating problems are very serious, but people can be helped with them. If you or anyone you know has an eating problem, it is important to tell someone about it. Talk to a doctor, a teacher, or someone you trust.

The most important way to stay healthy is to get enough exercise and eat a balanced diet. This means plenty of cereals and beans, fresh fruit and vegetables—and less fatty food.

Eat less fat!

Here are some tips to help you cut down on the amount of fat you eat:

1. Eat fewer fried foods. Choose grilled or steamed food instead of fried.
2. Eat less meat. Cut off the fat and any skin from the meat you eat.
3. Spread butter, margarine, or other spreads thinly, or change to a low-fat spread.
4. Eat fewer cookies, chocolate candies, and snacks like chips.
5. Change to low-fat milk.
6. Choose cheeses that are lower in fat, such as Edam, Gouda, Brie, Camembert, or cottage cheese.

Fill up with fiber!

You don't have to eat less just because you're cutting down on fats! You can fill up by eating more **fiber**.

Fiber is found in cereals, such as wheat, oats, and rice. This means foods made from these cereals, like oatmeal, whole wheat bread, and pasta (noodles), have lots of fiber. Other foods high in fiber are potatoes, beans, fresh fruits, and vegetables. And they all add up to a balanced diet!

ABOVE *Different people are different shapes and sizes. As long as you eat a balanced diet and exercise regularly, you will be the right shape for you.*

Glossary

Arteries The tubes that take blood from the heart to all parts of the body

Blood clot A clump of blood that sticks together and blocks an artery

Carbon dioxide One of the gases in the air we breathe

Cholesterol A type of fat that helps blood flow through our bodies

Diet The things a person eats

Energy Power made in your body from the food you eat and the chemicals in your body

Fiber A substance found in foods such as cereals. It fills you up and helps you digest your food.

Heart attack When the heart stops beating because it is not getting enough blood

Minerals Substances, such as calcium, that our bodies need to get from food

Monounsaturated fat An unsaturated fat that can be found in foods such as olive oil, avocadoes, and peanuts

Polyunsaturated fat An unsaturated fat that is found in foods such as vegetable oils

Processed Changing a food by adding ingredients, cooking it, freezing it, or treating it in some way

Protein A part of our diet that is needed by our bodies and is found in foods such as meat, milk, nuts

Saturated fat The kind of fat in meat, dairy products, coconut oil, and palm oil. It is usually solid.

Unsaturated fat The kind of fat that comes from most vegetables and nuts. It is usually soft or liquid.

Veins The tubes that take blood from all parts of the body back to the heart

Vitamins Substances, such as vitamin C, that our bodies need

Books to Read

About the Foods We Eat by Seymour Simon (McGraw-Hill Book Company, 1979)

Butter by Susan Wake (Carolrhoda Books, 1990)

Cheese by Linda Illsley (Carolrhoda Books, 1991)

Eggs by John Yates (Carolrhoda Books, 1989)

Food by David Marshall (Garrett Educational Corporation, 1991)

Health and Food by Dorothy Baldwin (Rourke Enterprises, 1987)

Meat by Elizabeth Clark (Carolrhoda Books, 1990)

Metric Chart

To find measurements that are almost equal

WHEN YOU KNOW:	MULTIPLY BY:	TO FIND:
AREA		
acres	0.41	hectares
WEIGHT		
ounces (oz.)	28.0	grams (g)
pounds (lb.)	0.45	kilograms (kg)
LENGTH		
inches (in.)	2.5	centimeters (cm)
feet (ft.)	30.0	centimeters
VOLUME		
teaspoons (tsp.)	5.0	milliliters (ml)
tablespoons (Tbsp.)	15.0	milliliters
fluid ounces (oz.)	30.0	milliliters
cups (c.)	0.24	liters (l)
quarts (qt.)	0.95	liters
TEMPERATURE		
Fahrenheit (°F)	0.56 (after subtracting 32)	Celsius (°C)

Index